1,000,000 Books

are available to read at

www.ForgottenBooks.com

Read online
Download PDF
Purchase in print

ISBN 978-1-5279-0542-9
PIBN 10916310

This book is a reproduction of an important historical work. Forgotten Books uses state-of-the-art technology to digitally reconstruct the work, preserving the original format whilst repairing imperfections present in the aged copy. In rare cases, an imperfection in the original, such as a blemish or missing page, may be replicated in our edition. We do, however, repair the vast majority of imperfections successfully; any imperfections that remain are intentionally left to preserve the state of such historical works.

Forgotten Books is a registered trademark of FB &c Ltd.
Copyright © 2018 FB &c Ltd.
FB &c Ltd, Dalton House, 60 Windsor Avenue, London, SW19 2RR.
Company number 08720141. Registered in England and Wales.

For support please visit www.forgottenbooks.com

1 MONTH OF FREE READING

at

www.ForgottenBooks.com

By purchasing this book you are eligible for one month membership to ForgottenBooks.com, giving you unlimited access to our entire collection of over 1,000,000 titles via our web site and mobile apps.

To claim your free month visit: www.forgottenbooks.com/free916310

* Offer is valid for 45 days from date of purchase. Terms and conditions apply.

English
Français
Deutsche
Italiano
Español
Português

www.forgottenbooks.com

Mythology Photography **Fiction**
Fishing Christianity **Art** Cooking
Essays Buddhism Freemasonry
Medicine **Biology** Music **Ancient Egypt** Evolution Carpentry Physics
Dance Geology **Mathematics** Fitness
Shakespeare **Folklore** Yoga Marketing
Confidence Immortality Biographies
Poetry **Psychology** Witchcraft
Electronics Chemistry History **Law**
Accounting **Philosophy** Anthropology
Alchemy Drama Quantum Mechanics
Atheism Sexual Health **Ancient History**
Entrepreneurship Languages Sport
Paleontology Needlework Islam
Metaphysics Investment Archaeology
Parenting Statistics Criminology
Motivational

CONSTITUTION

OF THE

BEVERLY YACHT CLUB,

WITH THE

BY-LAWS,

SAILING REGULATIONS, ETC.

"*Litus ama, altum alii teneant.*"

1892.

NEW YORK:
PRESS OF E. F. WEEKS, 45 WILLIAM STREET.

1892.

SG 85

Harvard College
APR 7 1897
Library.

Dr. S. A. Green

Officers of the Club.

1892.

Commodore,

H. P. BENSON.

Vice-Commodore,

GEORGE H. RICHARDS.

Secretary and Treasurer,

REGINALD C. ROBBINS.

Measurer,

W. LLOYD JEFFRIES.

REGATTA COMMITTEE.

N. H. EMMONS.	W. LLOYD JEFFRIES.
F. E. CABOT.	JOHN P. CUSHING.

ADMISSION COMMITTEE.

ROBERT SALTONSTALL.	F. W. SARGENT.
A. S. HARDY.	R. C. ROBBINS.
A. L. COCHRANE.	

SECRETARY'S ADDRESS:
403 WASHINGTON STREET, BOSTON, MASS.

LIST OF YACHTS.

Name.	Owner.	Keel or C.B.	Rig.	Racing Length.	Length over all.	Length on W.L.	Beam.	Draught.	Spar Measurements Heig't.	Base.	Gaff.	W.L. + Beam.	When Built.	Build'r.	Port.
ANONYMA	F. L. Dabney	C. B.	Cat	.....	28	2 23	9½ 11	2 2	.....	.....	.....	27 1	'90	7	7 12
ASHANTEE	G. H. Pillsbury	C. B.	Cat	.....	22	7 19	11¾ 9	.....	.....	.....	.....	23 3	'91	15	15 18
BOBOLINK	Ralph E. Forbes	C. B.	Sl'p	.....	20	18	7	2 4	.....	.....	.....	19	'79	28	28 19
BONITA	J. D. Parker	C. B.	Cat	.....	23	7 22	11 10	2 6	.....	.....	.....	25 4	'89	31	31 24
BONNIE BAIRN	George S. Fiske	Keel	Sl'p	.....	22	10 19	7	1 4	.....	.....	.....	19 9	'88	2	2 23
BUZZARD	A. B. Shepley	C. B.	Cat	.....	24	5 19	11½ 10	4	.....	.....	.....	23 8	'91	7	7 7
CARMI-A	C. H. W. Foster	Keel	Cut'r	.....	24	20	7	8 4	3	.....	.....	21 4	'83	9	9 10
CAT	Bruce Clark	C. B.	Cat	.....	18	6 16	4 8	4 1	6	.....	.....	19 3	'91	26	26 16
CAYUSE	F. W. Sargent	C. B.	Cat	.....	20	6 19	11 9	6 2	2	.....	.....	22 9	'90	22	22 12
CHAPOQUOIT	C. H. Jones	C. B.	Sl'p	.....	43	29	10 14	2	9	.....	.....	33 11	'92	22	22 17
CHARMION	Joshua Crane, Jr.	C. B.	Cat	.....	12	1 16	8⅛ 8	3½ 1	6	.....	.....	19 6	'90	29	29 25
COLUMBINE	Geo. A. Strong	Keel	Cut'r	.....	24	6 19	6 8	5	.....	.....	.....	21	'83	2	2
DAISY	Howard Stockton	C. B	Cat	.....	20	9 18	2 9	.....	.....	.....	.....	21 1	'88	7	7 12
DAISY	L. Loring	Keel	Cut'r	.....	32	25	8	6	.....	.....	.....	24 8	.....	.....	6

Name	Owner		Rig																	
DANDELION	C. F. Adams, 2d	C. B.	Cat	……	18	10	16	9	7	6	11	8	…	…	…	18	8	'75	3	9
DAWN	James M. Codman	Keel	Cat	……	17	…	…	…	…	1	10	…	…	…	…	…	…	…	…	12
DAWN	A. W. Baker	C. B.	Cat	……	20	8	18	4	8	5	11	…	…	…	…	20	8	…	…	6
DODGE	E. M. Padelford	Keel	Cat	……	14	…	12	4	3	…	…	…	…	…	…	12	…	'84	17	14
DOLLY	A. S. Hardy	C. B.	Cat	……	20	3	20	1	9	5	2	…	…	…	…	22	10	'82	22	15
DOLPHIN	Royal Robbins	C. B.	Cat	……	18	5	16	9	7	6	1	6	…	…	…	18	8	…	3	2
DORIS	J. Parkinson	C. B.	Cat	……	24	6	19	10	10	2	…	…	…	…	…	22	10	'92	22	15
DUCKLING	R. S. Hardy	C. B.	Cat	……	…	…	…	…	…	…	…	…	…	…	…	…	…	…	…	15
EDITH	G. G. Van Renssl'r	C. B.	Cat	……	17	4½	17	8	1	5	…	…	…	…	…	19	4	'88	33	18
ERL	W. E. C. Eustis	C. B.	Cat	……	15	…	…	…	…	…	…	…	…	…	…	…	…	'92	…	5
EINA	John Parkinson	C. B.	Cat	……	20	6	19	1	9	6	2	2	…	…	…	22	9	'89	22	12
ELSIE	H. H. Fay	C. B.	Cat	……	…	24	…	…	…	…	…	…	…	…	…	…	…	'84	18	8
FANCY	C. F. Lyman	Keel	Cut'r	……	41	29	9	9	7	3	…	…	…	…	…	28	10	'91	2	14
FIREFLY	R. L. Agassiz	C. B.	Cat	……	…	16	6	7	2	…	…	…	…	…	18	…	…	27	14
FREAK	J. B. Paine	Fin-Keel	J.& M	……	…	20	10	…	…	…	…	…	…	…	…	…	…	'92	16	2
GRAMPUS	W. E. C. Eustis	C. B.	Cat	……	30	6	23	9	12	1	2	8	…	…	…	22	9	'91	20	5
GYMNOTE	W. E. C. Eustis	C. B.	Cat	……	27	3	23	3	11	4	2	4	…	…	…	26	10	'89	7	5
HAMANA	S. D. Warren	C. B.	Cat	……	26	3	23	3	11	6	3	…	…	…	…	27	…	'89	15	18
HAWK	Gordon Dexter	C. B.	Sl'p	……	40	5	29	11	11	5	…	…	…	…	…	30	11	'90	2	3

LIST OF YACHTS.—Continued.

Name.	Owner.	Keel or C.B.	Rig.	Racing Length	Length over all	Length on W.L.	Beam.	Draught.	Heig't.	Base.	Gaff.	½ W.L. + Beam	When Built.	Builder.	Port.
Hera	Louis Bacon	C. B.	Cat		19 9¾	19 5½	9	2				21 11	'89	26	26 18
Hermione	R. L. Barstow	C. B.	Cat		20 2	19 10	9	9 2				23	'90	15	18
Heron	F. E. Cabot	C. B.	Cat		22 1	18	11							5	13
Hixie	R. W. Emmons	C. B.	Cat		26	19	9 10	1 2				23 3	'92	8	23
Hoiden	Gordon Dexter	C. B.	Slp		23 5	20	4 9	10				23 4	'79	6	3
Hoopoo	N. H. Emmons	C. B.	Cat		20 5	19	9 9	5 2				22 5	'90	4	23
Hornet	H. P. Benson	Keel	J.& M		28 6	20	7	6				20 4	'90	16	2
Iris	F. R. Bangs	C. B.	Cat		24 9	19	11 10	3 1				24 2	'81	11	12
Kathleen	R. S. Peabody	Keel	J.& M		27 3	19	11 7	10 4				21 3	'88	32	10
Kiowa	{ W. A. Jeffries / W. L. Jeffries }	C. B.	Cat		24 3	20	½ 9	10 2				23 2	'89	7	1
Kitten	{ G.H. Richards et als. }	C. B	Cat		17 5	17	8	7 2				19 11	'89	22	7
Koorali	R. C. Robbins	C. B.	Cat		25 6	20	6 10	2				23 8	'92	22	3
Kraken	Percy Chase	Keel	J.& M		28 5	20	8	7 5				21 11	'90	16	10
Lestris	Joshua Crane	C. B.	Cat		22 8	21	8 9	8 1	10			24 2	'80	12	5
Magpie	H. G. Otis	C. B.	Gt		20	19	10 9	7 2				22 10	'92	22	6

March—ioness	C. E. Hodges	C. B.	Cat	......	16	8	16	7	8	1	8	......	......	18	4	'91	. .	. .
Mar-guerite	F. Skinner, Jr.	Keel	Sl'p	......	26	7	23	9	9	8	1	8	......	......	24	10	'87	2	2
Mavis	James H. Proctor	Keel	Cut'r	......	32	. .	26	4	9	2	4	9	......	......	26	9	'82	2	3
Mildred	W. H. Wilkinson	Keel	Cut'r	......	42	. .	29	11	10	0	7	0	......	......	30	. .	'90	2	6
Mist	G. H. Lyman	C. B.	Cat	......	. .	. .	22	9	11	6	. .	......	......	26	8	'87	15	12
Moccasin	A. A. Beebe	C. B.	Cat	......	22	6	19	10	10	1½	2	2	......	......	24	. .	'91	30	23
Modoc	W. C. Loring	Keel	Cut'r	......	27	. .	22	7	. .	5	......	......	26	8	'84	2	6
Monomoy	F. C. Lowell	C. B.	Cat	......	. .	. .	12	. .	. .	. .	......	......	. .	. .	. .	. .	4
Myth	W. Burgess	C. B.	Cat	......	24	. .	23	6	9	9	2	......	......	25	5	'92	1	6
Nerissa	E. W. Codman	Keel	Sl'p	......	29	. .	23	8	. .	11	4	11	......	......	24	3	'88	2	2
Nina	F. C. Lowell	C. B	Cat	......	. .	. .	15	1	7	4	1	9	......	......	17	5	'75	14	4
Nixie	F. D. Cochrane	Keel	J.&M	......	24	7	20	2	7	1	11	. .	......	......	21	3	'86	16	3
Nomad	H. N. Richards	C. B.	Sl'p	......	31	9	29	12	. .	3	9	......	......	31	9	'77	28	5
Norna	F. C. Lowell	C. B.	Cat	......	22	. .	19	. .	. .	. .	......	......	. .	. .	'79	12	4
Nymph	Geo. G. Amory	C. B.	Cat	......	16	. .	15	10	7	3	. .	......	......	17	9	......	24	12
Olga	John L. Gardner	C. B.	Cat	......	20	6	17	9	. .	. .	......	......	. .	. .	'75	10	22
Oswa	S. C. Davis	Keel	Cut'r	......	. .	. .	. .	. .	. .	5	......	......	. .	11	. .	. .	26
Owl	F. Dexter	Keel	Cut'r	......	29	6	20	10	8	. .	. .	......	......	21	11	'92	2	3

LIST OF YACHTS.—*Continued.*

Name.	Owner.	Keel or C. B.	Rig.	Racing Length	Length over all	Length on W. L.	Beam	Draught	Heig't	Base	Gaff	½W.L.+Beam	When Built	Builder	Port.
Paradox	L. M. Clark	C. B.	Cat	.....	19 5	17 1	8	3 1	9			19 8	'79	16	21
Petrel	G. H. Richards	C. B.	Cat	.....	18 4	18 3	8	5				20 7	'85	22	7
Pixy	F. W. Chandler	C. B.	Cat	.....	22	19 3	9	2	6			21 10	'86	25	10
Psyche	Francis Gray	C. B.	Cat	.....	19 11½	16 9½	8	3 1	5			19 5	'77	6	21
Puzzle	W. Amory, 2d	C. B.	Cat	.....	20	5 19	9 9	7 2	2			22 9	'90	22	12
Queen Mab	W. O. Gay	C. B.	Cat	.....	24	6 21	10 10	3 2	6			24 10	'72	6	6
Ramona	Wm. Sheafe	C. B.	Cat	.....	27	8 25	6 11	3 3				28 9	'88	23	12
Rana	H. N. Richards	C. B.	Cat	.....	12	6 12	6	1	6			14 5	'91	24	5
Reaper	H. P. Benson	Fin-Keel	J.&M	.....	31	20	10 6	9 6	6			20 10	'92	3	10
Rip	C. B. Jefferson	C. B.	Cat	.....	19 ½	15	9 8	7				19 1	'90	7	7
Rita	H. B. Richardson	C. B.	Cat	.....	18	18	9 8	1	6			20 6	'79	21	1
Sachem	J. S. Fay, Jr.	C. B.	Cat	.....	20	20	10	3				23 4	'85	12	8
Samaria	G. L. Peabody	C. B.	Cat	.....	16	16	10 8	3 1	10			19 6	.....	6	20
Scorpion	John L. Gardner	Keel	Cut'r	.....	23	23	8	3	6			23 4	'80	6	22
Scup	J. T. Coolidge, Jr.	C. B.	Cat	.....	.....	12	5 5	6				13 8	.....	19	4

Name	Owner											
SIRIUS	{ W. C. Bray, / M. N. Bray, }	C. B.	Cat	..	26	11 24	10 11	..	..	..	6 ..	22 12
SPORT	W. C. Appleton, 2d	C. B.	Cat	..	16	7 16	6 6	..	..	17	'86	21 13
SQUALL	J. G. Palfrey	C. B.	Cat	..	17	7 16	11 8	7 1	8	..	'91	7 16
STAR	{ M. N. Bray, / W. C. Bray, }	C. B.	Cat	..	20	3 18	2 8	6	..	20	7 '88	7 12
SUKEY	George C. Adams	C. B.	Cat	..	21	11 18	4 8	1 10	..	20	3 '82	5 9
SURPRISE	Jas. M. Codman	C. B.	Cat	..	24	6 23	11½ 11	3½ 2	..	27	4 '84	22 12
SYLPH	Aug. Hemenway	C. B.	Cat	..	..	16	9 7	4 1	6	18	6 ..	3 6
TANTRUM	Wm. Amory, 2d	C. B.	Cat	..	..	22	1 10	4½ 2	5	25	'83	22 12
TIGRESS	F. R. Sears, Jr.	C. B.	Cat	..	29	23	11 11	2 6	..	27	1 '90	7 3
TOM CAT	W. C. Loring	C. B.	Cat	..	20	6 19	10 10	2	..	23	2 ..	.. 3
TONY	C. B. Jefferson	C. R.	Cat	..	..	..	..	..	..	..	'88	7 15
TYCOON	J. L. Stackpole	C. B.	Cat	..	20	3 19	9 9	11	..	23	1 '91	15 18
VIOLET	{ G. H. Richards / et als. }	C. B.	Cat	..	24	10 24	5 11	3 2	3	27	6 '82	12 7
WANDA	R. C. Robbins	C. B	Cat	..	23	7 20	9 8	11 3	..	24	1 '87	2 3
WHISPER	A. R. Weld	C. B.	Cat	..	27	5 24	5 11	10 2	9	28	'83	11 12
WIDGEON	M. Williams, Jr.	C. B.	Cat	..	24	4 23	6 11	2 2	4	26	10 '89	7 15
WITCH	B. B. Crowninsh'ld	Keel	Cut'r	..	26	22	8 8	5	..	23	1 '89	25 10
YANKEE DOODLE	Joseph Azarian	C. B.	Cat	..	26	23	11	2 2	..	26	4 '80	6 11
ZINGARA	E. V. Bird	C. B.	Sl'p	..	29	1 24	3 11	20 3	9	28	6 '84	15 18

LIST OF YACHTS.—Continued.

Name.	Owner.	Keel or C.B.	Rig.	Racing Length.	Length over all.	Length on W.L.	Beam.	Draught.	Spar Measurements			¾ W.L. + Beam.	When Built.	Builder.	Port.
									Heig't.	Base.	Gaff.				
Building	A. Hemenway	C. B.	J.& M.	....	25	6 20	11 10	1 5	....	....	....	24 6	'92	2	2 6
Building	W. H. Davis	C. B.	Cat	....	....	....	....	....	....	....	....	....	'92	26	16
Building	J. W. Jefferson	C. B.	Cat	....	19 6	15	10 8	1 8	....	....	....	19 2	'91	7	15
Building	L. M. Stockton	Fin-Keel	Cat	....	....	19	11	....	....	....	....	....	'92	..	12
Building	C. H. W. Foster	Keel	J.& M.	....	....	20	10	....	....	....	....	....	'92	2	2 10

Racing Length means that north of the Cape. No boats have yet been measured under the new rule.

LIST OF YACHTS OWNED BY MEMBERS OF THE CLUB, BUT TOO LARGE TO ENTER THE RACES.

Name.	Rig	Owner.	Port.	Tonnage. Old.	Tonnage. New.	Length over all.	Length on Water Line.	Beam.	Depth.	Draught.	C. B. or Keel.
Alborak	Sl'p	J. B. Paine	Nahant				46	14 2	10 2½	8	Keel
Alga	Cut'r	C. A. Longfellow	Nahant			56	45	14		6 3	Keel
Alice	Sl'p	C. A. Longfellow	Nahant	68.27	32.78	66 6	59 8	17 6	6 3	6 4	Keel
Baboon	Cut'r	G. A. Goddard	Boston			52	39 6	13		8 3	Keel
Barbara	Cut'r	C. H. W. Foster	Marblehead			62	45 9	13		11 8	Keel
Beatrix	Sl'p	C. F. & G.C. Adams	Cohasset				45 6				C. B.
Chiquita	Cut'r	Aug. Hemenway	Boston			49	39 6	13		7	C. B.
Dagmar	St'mr	H. H. Fay	Boston	88.08	52.72	110	97	16 6	9 4	7 6	Keel
Edith	Cut'r	F. F. Emery, Jr.	Boston		13.87	49	42 6	10		7	Keel
Foam	Sch'r	Arthur Dexter	Boston	102.1	64.95	88	82 6	21	7	7 6	C. B.
Fortuna	Sch'r	H. S. Hovey	Gloucester	194.75	80.83	109	95 6	22	12 8	12	Keel
Gossip	Cut'r	H. B. Richardson	New York			55	39 8	12 8		9 6	Keel
Gossoon	Cut'r	C. F. Adams, 2d / Geo. C. Adams	Cohasset			53	39 10	12		7 6	Keel
Hannibl	St'mr	C. H. W. Foster	Boston			97	85	15 1		8	Keel

LIST OF YACHTS OWNED BY MEMBERS OF THE CLUB, BUT TOO LARGE TO ENTER THE RACES.—Continued.

Name	Rig	Owner	Port	Tonnage Old	Tonnage New	Length over all	Length on Water Line	Beam	Depth	Draught	C. B. or Keel
Ien	Sl'p	E. T. Scott	Bar Harbor			54	39 11	12 6	8 6	10 6	Keel
Hira	Sl'p	H. N. Richards	Met			41		11		7 2	Keel
Hilda	Cut'r	C. P. Curtis	Swampscott			38 7	31 5	18		6 11	Keel
Kathleen	Sch'r	E. A. Bangs	Boston		34	68	58	16 9	6 3	8 6	Keel
Lotus	Sch'r	Daniel Appleton	New York	52.72	20 51	63 11	59	23 6	9	10 4	C. B.
Mayflower	Sch'r	W. A. Gardner	Beverly			97	85 7	23		11 6	Keel
Mohican	Sch'r	H. D. Burnham	Stonington	242	114.27	119 10	106 8	11 6		6 1	Keel
Nid	Sl'p	W. O. Gay	Boston			38 6	34	15	5	4 6	C. B.
North Star	Sl'p	M. K. Abbott	Boston		15 2	47 9	43 1	13 11			C. B.
Ramona	Sl'p	{ M. N. Bray, W. C. Bray }	Wareham			35 9	33	12 11		5	C. B.
Reli Me	Sl'p	N. H. Emmons	Falmouth			39 1	33 10	14 2		5 4	C. B.
Shadow	Sl'p	John Bryant	Cohasset	18 34	12.86	36 9	33 6	5 9		5	Keel
Shona	Cut'r	Chas. H. Tweed	Beverly		5	42 9	33 1	7 9	4	2 9	Keel
Spruce	St'mr	J. L. Gardner	Roque Island		4.75	35 9	31				

12

								C. B.
VOLUNTEER...	Sch'r	Chas. J. Paine.	Boston	......	118	89 6	23 2	10	......	Keel
WAIF	Sl'p	Gov. Kortright.....	Bristol......	......	39	35	11	......	6 6	Keel
WHITE WING	Cut'r	Robert Saltonstall..	Beverly......	......	39	32 5	8 5	......	6 9	Keel
ZIGEUNER.....	Sl'p	R. L. Agassiz, Max Agassiz,	Newport ...	......	50 9	42	12 1	8	8	Keel
Buil dig.....	St'mr	J. P. Cushing	Bverly......	......	50	......	......	......	......	Keel

LIST OF BUILDERS.

1. R. W. Bibber...................................South Boston.
2. George Lawley & Son.........................South Boston.
3. J. B. Herreshoff ....Bristol, R. I.
4. S. B. Eldridge..................................New Bedford.
5. W. F. Mayberry................................Quincy.
6. Pierce Brothers................................South Boston.
7. Frederick J. Dunn ....Monument Beach.
8. Chas. Gifford ....Vineyard Haven.
9. J. H. Keating...................................Marblehead.
10. John Rock......................................Beverly.
11. J. Washburne ....Wareham.
12. D. & C. H. Crosby............................Osterville.
13. Samuel Damon................................New Bedford.
14. —— Smith....................................Mystic, Conn.
15. A. M. Jenney..................................Mattapoisett.
16. W. B. Smith ....South Boston.
17. J. F. Smith.....................................New York.
18. H. C. Lumbert.................................Hyannis.
19. C. A. Borden..................................South Boston.
20. H. M. Crosby..................................Osterville.
21. A. O Higgins..................................Cohasset.
22. C. C. Hanley..................................Monument.
23. T. D. Stoddard................................Newport.
24. C. A. Clark....................................Bird Island.
25. William Eddy..................................Marblehead.
26. Eben Holmes..................................Marion.
27. —— Barlow ....Newport.
28. J. F. Mumm ....Brooklyn.
29. Owner ——
30. W. Crosby....................................Osterville.
31. W. V. Read...................................Fall River.
32. —— McPhail................................East Boston.
33. Jabez Jenney.................................Marion.

LIST OF PORTS.

Swampscott.................... 1	Newport.........................14
Nahant........................ 2	Bourne 15
Beverly....................... 3	Marion 16
Cotuit........................ 4	West Falmouth..................17
Cataumet...................... 5	Mattapoisett...................18
Boston........................ 6	Naushon........................19
Monument Beach................ 7	Salem..........................20
Wood's Holl................... 8	Dorchester 21
Quincy........................ 9	Roque Island, Me...............22
Marblehead....................10	Falmouth.......................23
Constantinople................11	Quissett.......................24
Wareham.......................12	Pocassett 25
Cohasset......................13	Magnolia.......................26

MEMBERS

OF THE

BEVERLY YACHT CLUB.

Abbott, M. K.
Adams, C. F., 2d.
Adams, George C.
Agassiz, Max.
Agassiz, R. L.
Amory, C. W.
Amory, Geo. G.
Amory, William, 2d.
Appleton, Daniel.
Appleton, William W.
Appleton, William C., 2d.
Azarian, Joseph.

Bacon, Louis.
Baker, Arthur M.
Bangs, Edward A.
Bangs, F. Reginald.
Barstow, R. L.
Beebe, Arthur A.
Benson, H. P.
Bird, E. V.
Bliss, C. W., Jun.

Boardman, T. Dennie.
Bray, M. N.
Bray, W. C.
Brimmer, Martin.
Bryant, John.
Burgess, Sidney W.
Burgess, Walter.
Burnham, Henry D.

Cabot, F. Elliott.
Chandler, F. W.
Chase, Percy.
Clark, Bruce.
Clark, Louis M.
Cobb, John C.
Cochrane, A. L.
Cochrane, F. D.
Codman, Edward W.
Codman, James M.
Codman, Philip.
Codman, Richard.
Coolidge, J. T.

Coolidge, T. Jefferson, Jun.
Crane, Joshua.
Crane, Joshua, Jun.
Crowninshield, B. B.
Curtis, Charles P.
Cushing, John P.

Dabney, F. L.
Dabney, L. S.
Daland, Tucker.
Davis, S. C.
Davis, Wm. H.
Dexter, Arthur.
Dexter, Franklin.
Dexter, F. Gordon.
Dexter, Gordon.

Edmands, T. S.
Ellis, Edward C.
Emery, F. F., Jun.
Emmons, N. H.
Emmons, R. W.,
Eustis, W. E. C.

Fay, Henry H.
Fay, Jos. S., Jun.
Fiske, Geo. S.
Forbes, Ralph E.
Foster, C. H. W.

Gardner, John L.
Gardner, W. A.
Gay, W. O.
Goddard, George A.

Grant, Patrick, Jun.
Gray, Francis.

Hardy, A. H.
Hardy, A. S.
Hardy, Roger S.
Haven, Edward B.
Heard, John (Hon.).
Hemenway, Augustus.
Hodges, C. E.
Hovey, Henry S.

Iasigi, Joseph A.
Inches, George B.

Jefferson, C. B.
Jefferson, J. W.
Jeffries, John.
Jeffries, Walter Lloyd.
Jeffries, William A.
Jones, Chas. H.

Kortright, Gouverneur.

Lawrence, William P.
Longfellow, Charles A.
Loring, Lindsley.
Loring, W. C.
Lowell, F. C.
Lyman, C. F.
Lyman George H.

Otis, H. G.

Padelford, E. M.

Paine, Charles J.
Paine, John B.
Palfrey, J. G.
Parker, J. D.
Parkinson, John.
Peabody, George L.
Peabody, L. R.
Peabody, R. S.
Pickman, Dudley L.
Pillsbury, G. H.
Prince, Chas. A.
Prince, Morton.
Proctor, James H.
Proctor, Thomas E.

Rantoul, A. N.
Richards, George H.
Richards, H. N.
Richardson, H. B
Robbins, Royal.
Robbins, R. C.
Russell, E. B.

Saltonstall, Robert.
Sargent, Francis W.
Scott, E. T.
Sears, Fred. R., Jun.
Sears, H. M.

Shaw, H. R.
Sheafe, Wm.
Shepley, Arthur B.
Skinner, Francis, Jun.
Sohier, William D.
Stackpole, J. L.
Stackpole, J. L., Jun.
Stockton,. Howard.
Stockton, Lawrence M.
Stockton, Philip.
Strong, G. A.

Taylor, W. O.
Thayer, E. V. R.
Thomas, Isaac R.
Tweed, Charles H.

Van Rensselaer, G. G.

Warren, S. D.
Waterhouse, W. E.
Weld, Alfred R.
Weld, E. M.
Weld, Stephen M.
Wheelright, A. W.
Whitney, Edward F. (Hon.)
Wilkinson, W. H.
Williams, Hugh.
Williams, Moses, Jun.
Wright, Eben.

CONSTITUTION.

OF THE

BEVERLY YACHT CLUB.

ARTICLE I.

NAME.

The name of this Club shall be THE BEVERLY YACHT CLUB.

ARTICLE II.

OFFICERS.

The officers of the Club shall be a Commodore, Vice-Commodore, Secretary, who shall also act as Treasurer, and a Measurer. There shall also be a Regatta Committee, consisting of five members; the Measurer may appoint one or more assistants.

ARTICLE III.

ELECTION OF OFFICERS.

The officers of the Club shall be elected at the Annual Meeting, which shall be held on the Second Friday in December; they shall each be elected on a separate ballot, and shall hold office for one year. Vacancies may be filled at any meeting, notice having been sent to each member at least one week previous to such meeting.

ARTICLE IV.

DUTY OF COMMODORE.

It shall be the duty of the Commodore to take command of the squadron, and to preside at all meetings. He may call a meeting of the Club at his pleasure, and shall do so at the request of three members, two of whom shall be owners of yachts.

ARTICLE V.

DUTY OF VICE-COMMODORE.

It shall be the duty of the Vice-Commodore to assist the Commodore in the discharge of his duties, and to officiate in his absence.

ARTICLE VI.

DUTY OF SECRETARY.

It shall be the duty of the Secretary :

To keep a record of the proceedings of all meetings of the Club in a book provided for that purpose.

To keep a correct roll of all the members.

To keep a list of the name, dimensions, rig, and ownership of each yacht enrolled in the Club.

To notify members elect of their election, and to notify each member of every meeting and regatta.

To have Club-books printed, as provided by the By-Laws.

To prepare a report of each regatta, to be sent to one or more papers for publication.

ARTICLE VII.

DUTY OF TREASURER.

It shall be the duty of the Treasurer to receive all moneys due the Club, and pay all bills contracted by it ; keeping a correct account of the same in a book provided for that purpose.

To make a report at each meeting of the receipts and expenditures of the Club.

ARTICLE VIII.

DUTY OF MEASURER.

It shall be the duty of the Measurer to measure all yachts enrolled in the Club, and report their measurements to the Secretary.

ARTICLE IX.

DUTY OF REGATTA COMMITTEE.

It shall be the duty of the Regatta Committee to arrange all regattas, and to appoint one or more persons to act, together with the members of the committee, as judges for the same.

ARTICLE X.

ELECTION OF MEMBERS.

The election of members shall be by a committee, which shall be appointed by the Commodore, consisting of three owners of Yachts, and two who are not owners ; a quorum being two of the former and one of the latter. The name of the proposed member, with the name of the proposer and seconder, shall be forwarded to the committee. Two black balls shall exclude.

The committee shall have full power to fill any vacancies which may occur in their number.

ARTICLE XI.

VOTING.

Upon questions directly affecting the Sailing Regulations and the government of yachts and regattas, only yacht owners shall vote ; each yacht being represented by one owner.

At the election of officers, and upon all other questions, each member shall have one vote.

ARTICLE XII.

AMENDMENT.

This constitution may be amended at any meeting, but no amendment shall be valid until approved at a subsequent meeting.

BY-LAWS.

CHAPTER I.

DUES.

Each member, on his election, shall pay the sum of ten dollars, which shall include his dues for the current year; if such sum is not paid by the end of the fiscal year, such election shall be null and void. Each subsequent annual payment shall be five dollars, and shall become due at the Annual Meeting of each year.

Members who are absent from the United States during the whole fiscal year, commencing on the Second Friday in December, shall be exempt from their dues for such year, provided they give notice of their intended absence to the Secretary.

On the first day of November the Secretary shall notify each member whose dues for the year remain unpaid, unless in case of absence; and, if any member allows his dues for the year to remain unpaid, he shall be considered to have forfeited his membership.

No member shall be entitled to any of the privileges of the Club until his dues are paid.

CHAPTER II.

QUORUM.

Ten members shall constitute a quorum for the transaction of business.

CHAPTER III.

YACHT SQUADRON.

Any yacht not measuring more than thirty feet on the water-line, owned by a member or members of the Club, may be enrolled in the yacht squadron upon the owner or owners filing with the Secretary a description of the yacht.

CHAPTER IV.

CLUB SIGNALS.

The signal of the Club shall be a pointed burgee, its width being two-thirds of its length; the device, a red five-pointed star, in diameter one-quarter the greatest width of the signal, placed in the middle of a white triangle whose base is the luff of the signal, the apex being in the middle of the triangle, dis.ant one-half the length of the same from the luff; the rest of the flag blue.*

CHAPTER V.

PENDANTS.

The Commodore, when afloat, will wear a broad pendant with a foul anchor surrounded by thirteen five-pointed stars in white on a blue field.

The Vice-Commodore will wear a broad pendant with the same device on a red field.

CHAPTER VI.

PROXIES.

Voting may be by proxy.

CHAPTER VII.

NOTICES.

Notices of the annual meeting shall be sent to every member at least six days previous to the meeting; of all special meetings, at least three days before such meetings; and of all regattas, at least six days before such regattas.

---

*Signals may be obtained of R. M. Yale, 29 South Market Street, Boston, or I. W. Wheeler & Co., 64 Commercial Street, Boston.

CHAPTER VIII.

SPECIAL MEETINGS.

Nothing shall be acted on at a special meeting, except business stated in the call for the meeting.

CHAPTER IX.

CHANGE OF OWNERSHIP.

Each member, upon buying or selling a yacht, shall give notice of the same to the Secretary.

CHAPTER X.

EXPULSIONS.

In case of any occurrence injurious to the welfare of the Club, the name or names of any member or members implicated therein may be removed from the list of members by a vote of the majority of the members present at any meeting.

CHAPTER XI.

CLUB BOOKS.

There shall be printed each year, under the direction of the Secretary, a book for the use of the members of the Club, containing the Constitution, By-Laws, and Sailing Regulations, together with a list of members, and also of the yachts belonging to the Club, with their dimensions, rig and ownership, as well as a chart of their private signals and the Club flags, and an account of the races sailed the previous season.

CHAPTER XII.

AMENDMENTS.

These By-Laws may be amended at any regular meeting, or at a special meeting, if proposed alteration is included in the call for the meeting.

SAILING REGULATIONS.

RULE I.

MANAGEMENT OF RACES.

All races, and yachts sailing therein, shall be under the direction of the Regatta Committee of the Club. All matters shall be subject to their approval and control, and all doubts, questions, and disputes which may arise shall be subject to their decision. Their decisions shall be based upon these rules, so far as they apply, but as no rules can be devised capable of meeting every incident and accident of sailing, the Regatta Committee shall keep in view the ordinary customs of the sea, and discourage all attempts to win a race by other means than fair sailing and superior speed and skill. The decisions of the Committee shall be final.

RULE II.

APPLICATION.

Yachts entered in a race shall be amenable to these Rules from the time the preparatory signal is given.

These rules shall apply to all yachts sailing in a race, whether in the same or in different classes.

All yachts belonging to the Club, not sailing in a race, shall keep out of the way of yachts in the race, and to leeward of them.

RULE III.

POSTPONEMENT.

The Regatta Committee shall have power to postpone any race, should unfavorable weather render such a course desirable.

RULE IV.

CLASSIFICATION AND MEASUREMENT FOR RACES NORTH OF CAPE COD.

North of Cape Cod, the classification shall be as follows: 1st class: all yachts over 25 feet water-line and not over 30 feet water-line. 2d class: all yachts over 21 feet water-line and not over 25 feet water-line 3d class: all yachts over 18 feet water-line and not over 21 feet water-line. Third class Cats and third class Sloops shall sail for separate prizes. 4th class: all yachts of 18 feet water-line and under.

Racing Measurement North of Cape Cod shall be as follows:

The water-line length shall be taken from point of immersion forward, to point of immersion aft. In cases where any portion of the rudder or rudder-post projects above the water, such portion shall not be included in the water-line length.

The crew need not be aboard, but if aboard must be stationed amidships.

The sail area is to be ascertained by taking a perpendicular along the after side of the mainmast, from the underside of gaff-topsail block or sheave on topmast, to the upper side of boom, when resting on the saddle, or on the lowest part of goose neck; the distance of which point from the main deck or house deck is to be recorded by the Measurer, together with the other points used in measurement. In all yachts, the forward point of measurement of the base-line shall be midway between the intersection of the bowsprit and jib topsail stay, and the centre of the tack cringle of the jib or flying jib, when set. In all cases where the extreme length of the spinnaker boom exceeds the distance from the forward side of the forward mast to the forward point of measurement, such excess shall be added to the base-line. The after point of measurement shall be the end of the main boom in schooners, cutters and sloops, and of the mizzen boom in yawls. The main topmast shall be measured from the hounds of the lower mast to the lower side of the topsail halyard block or sheave, and eighty per cent. of this length shall be taken from the extreme length of the main gaff measured from the inside of the jaws, to the after end, the remainder of the gaff being added to the base-line, as measured above. The area from these figures is obtained by multiplying the corrected base by the perpendicular, and dividing by two. To the square root of the area, as ascertained, add the water-line length, and divide the product by two. The result is the measurement for time allowance.

In measuring boats without topmasts, the perpendicular is to be measured to the highest point of attachment of the uppermost halyard block on the mast, and in such boats the point of attachment of the throat halyard block shall be the point of measurement, corresponding to the hounds. In measuring boats without head sails, the after side of the forward mast is to be taken as the forward point of the base line.

The Measurer, at the time of making his measurement, shall make a distinctive mark at each end of the water-line.

RULE V.

CLASSIFICATION AND MEASUREMENT FOR RACES SOUTH OF CAPE COD.

Classification: First class: all yachts over 24 feet water-line and not over 30 feet water-line. Second class: all yachts over 20 feet water-line and not over 24 feet water-line. Third class: all yachts over 17 feet water-line and not over 20 feet water-line. Fourth class: all yachts of 17 feet water-line and under.

Racing measurement South of Cape Cod shall be two-thirds the water-line length plus the extreme beam.

The water-line length shall be measured when the yacht is afloat, and in her ordinary trim, with two men aboard, who shall be stationed, as near as possible, at a distance of two-thirds of the water-line length from the bow. Also,

The anchor shall be on board, sail furled and boom in the crotch. If a centre board yacht, the centre board shall be hauled up so that the lower edge of the centre board shall be flush with the keel.

This length shall be taken from the point of immersion forward to the point of immersion aft; but in case any portion of the rudder or rudder-post comes above the surface of the water, such part shall not be included in the water-line length.

RULE VI.
SAILS.

Yachts in third and fourth classes north of Cape Cod, and catboat classes south of Cape Cod, contending for prizes, may carry sails as follows: Schooners, mainsail, foresail, forestaysail and jib; Sloops and Cutters, mainsail, forestaysail and jib; Catboats, mainsail. In other classes there shall be no restriction in regard to sails, unless otherwise ordered by the Regatta Committee, who shall have full power to regulate this; *and no means except sails* shall be used to propel a yacht and no spinnaker shall be carried extending above the upper halliard sheave or block.

RULE VII.
ALLOWANCE OF MEN.

Yachts during a regatta are allowed to carry one man for every five feet of length on water-line, and fractional part thereof.

RULE VIII.
MEMBERS ON EACH YACHT.

Every yacht competing for a prize shall be sailed only by a member of the Club.

RULE IX.

BALLAST.

No change in the weight of ballast shall be made on the day of a race, and no trimming by dead weight allowed during a race in any class.

RULE X.

SPARS.

No change of spars shall be made on the day of a race, except in case of accident; in which case notice of the change shall be given to the Regatta Committee before the preparatory signal, and the new spars shall be of the same length as those for which they are substituted.

RULE XI.

INSTRUCTIONS.

Each yacht entered for a race shall, at the time of entry, or as soon after as possible, be supplied with written or printed instructions as to the conditions of the race, the course to be sailed, marks, etc. Nothing shall be considered as a mark in the course unless especially named in such instructions.

The Regatta Committee shall have power to change the course, or amend the instructions, on or before the day of the race, providing notice of such change is given to each yacht before the preparatory signal is made.

RULE XII.

TIME OF RACE.

Yachts in the first and second classes must sail the race at the rate of two and three-quarter miles an hour; those in other classes at the rate of two and a-half miles an hour.

RULE XIII.

ANCHORING.

Yachts may anchor during a race without forfeiting their claim to a prize, but must weigh their anchors on again resuming their course.

RULE XIV.

REMOVAL OF STAKEBOAT.

Should any stakeboat, buoy, or other mark be absent or moved from its proper position during a race, the question of re-sailing the race shall be decided by the Regatta Committee.

RULE XV.

ACCIDENTS.

In case of accident to another vessel, or of a man falling overboard from another vessel, all yachts in a position to do so shall use their utmost endeavors to render assistance, and if it should appear, in the judgment of the Regatta Committee, that any yacht so rendering assistance was thereby prevented from winning the race, the committee shall have power to order the race to be re-sailed between such yacht and the actual winner in the same class.

RULE XVI.

START AND FINISH.

§ 1. The time of the start and finish shall be taken when the point marked by the foremast in schooners, and the mainmast in single-masted vessels and yawls, crosses the given line; but if this point in any yacht be across the line when the signal for the start in her class is made, she must return and re-cross the line.

§ 2. A yacht so returning, or one working into position from the wrong side of the line after the signal for the start has been made, must keep clear of, and give way to, all competing yachts.

RULE XVII.

§1. When one yacht is approaching another yacht so as to involve risk of fouling, one of them shall keep clear of the other as follows:

§ 2. A yacht free shall keep clear of one close-hauled.

§ 3. When both yachts are close-hauled, or both free, or both have the wind aft and have the wind on opposite sides, the yacht with the wind on the port side shall keep clear.

§ 4. When both yachts are free, or both have the wind aft and have the wind on the same side, the yacht to windward shall keep clear.

§ 5. A yacht with the wind aft is deemed to have the wind on the side opposite to that on which she is carrying her main boom. A yacht with the wind aft shall keep clear of a yacht on any other point of sailing.

§ 6. An overtaking yacht shall in every case, as long as an overlap exists, keep clear of the yacht which is being overtaken.

§ 7. An overlap is established when an overtaking yacht has no longer a free choice on which side she will pass, and continues to exist as long as the leeward yacht by luffing or the weather yacht by bearing away is in danger of fouling.

§ 8. When of two yachts one is obliged to keep clear, the other shall not so alter her course as to involve risk of fouling.

§ 9. A yacht may luff as she pleases in order to prevent another from passing her to windward, provided she begins to luff before an overlap has been established.

§ 10. A yacht shall not bear away out of her course so as to hinder another in passing to leeward.

§ 11. A yacht shall not become entitled to her rights on a new course until she has filled away.

§ 12. When two yachts, both close-hauled on the same tack, are converging by reason of the leeward yacht holding a better wind, and neither can claim the rights of a yacht being overtaken, then the yacht to leeward shall keep clear.

§ 13. If an overlap exists between two yachts when both of

them without tacking are about to pass a mark on the required side, then the outside yacht must give the inside yacht room to pass clear of the mark. A yacht shall not, however, be justified in attempting to establish an overlap and thus force a passage between another yacht and the mark after the latter has altered her helm for the purpose of rounding.

§ 14. A mark is any vessel, boat, buoy or other object used to indicate the course and does not in the preceding section involve any question of sea-room.

§ 15. When a yacht is in danger of running aground, or of touching a pier, rock or other obstruction, and cannot go clear by altering her course, without fouling another yacht, then the latter shall, on being hailed by the former, at once give room ; and in case one yacht is forced to tack or bear away, in order to give room, the other shall also tack, or bear away, as the case may be, at as near the same time as is possible without danger of fouling.

RULE XVIII.

DISQUALIFICATION.

§ 1. A yacht touching a mark or causing a mark-boat to shift her position, unless wrongfully compelled to do so by another yacht, shall be disqualified.

§ 2. If a yacht, in consequence of a violation of any of these Rules, shall foul another yacht, or compel another yacht to foul any yacht, mark or obstruction, or to run aground, she shall be disqualified and shall pay all damages ; and any yacht which shall wrongfully cause another to alter her course in order to avoid fouling, or shall, without due cause, compel another yacht to give room, under § 15 of Rule XVI, or shall herself fail to tack or bear away, as required by that Section, or shall in any other way infringe or fail to comply with any of these Rules, shall be disqualified.

RULE XIX.

§ 1. All protests against any yacht in a race must be made in writing to the Regatta Committee or Judges, within half an hour after the close of the race.

§ 2. The Committee may also, without a protest, disqualify any yacht should it come to their knowledge that she has committed a breach of the Rules.

§ 3. All questions arising in any race, not covered by these Rules, shall be decided by the Committee.

§ 4. The decisions of the Committee shall be final, unless they see fit to refer any questions at issue for the decision of the Club.

RULE XX.

AMENDMENTS.

These sailing regulations may be amended at any general or special meeting, provided notice of the proposed amendment has been given in the call for the meeting.

RACES FOR 1892.

The dates for races at Monument Beach will be as follows:

June 17th, 1st Open Sweepstakes.

July 4th, 2d Open Sweepstakes.

July 16th, 1st B. B. Championship.

July 30th, 3d Open Sweepstakes.

Aug. 20th, 2d B. B. Championship.

Sept. 3d, 4th Open Sweepstakes.

Sept. 5th,   Open Race.

Sept. 17th, 3d B. B. Championship.

Committee reserves right to change order of Races by giving due notice.

Dates for Open and "21-footer" races at *Marblehead* will be announced.

COURSES AT MARBLEHEAD.

For 1st and 2d Classes.

No 1.—Leaving Red Buoy No. 6 on starboard ; Bowditch's Ledge Beacon on starboard ; Red Buoy No. 2 on Gales Ledge on starboard ; S. E. Breaker Buoy on starboard ; Halfway Rock on starboard ; Black Buoys No. 1 and 3 on port ; to Judge's Yacht. 10½ miles.

No. 2.—Reverse of No. 1.

* No. 3.—Leaving Black Buoys No. 3 and 1, Halfway Rock and Can Buoy off S. E. Pig Breaker on starboard ; Roaring Bull, Tinker's Island, Tom Moore's Rock and Black Buoys 1 and 3 on port, to Judge's Yacht. 10 miles.

* No. 4.—Reverse of No. 3.

For 3d and 4th Classes.

No. 5.—Leaving R. Buoy No. 6 on starboard, Stakeboat just N. of Bowditch's Ledge Beacon and Stakeboat off Curtis' Point, on port ; B. Buoys, 7, 5 and 3 and Selman's Berth Buoy on starboard, and return. 7½ miles.

No. 6.—Reverse of No, 5.

No. 7.—Leaving B. Buoy 3, Archer's Rock Buoy, Cat Island.

---

* If S. E. Pig Breaker Can Buoy is not in place, the Spar Buoy shall be rounded in its place.

Martin's Rock Buoy and Halfway Rock on Starboard, B. Buoys 1 and 3 on port, and return. 6⅜ miles.

No. 8.—Reverse of No. 7.

COURSES AT MONUMENT BEACH.

No. 1.—From starting point, leaving Black Buoy No. 3 on starboard, Bird Island Buoy No. 13 on port, Scraggy Neck Buoy No. 10 on port, to Judge's Yacht. 10¼ miles.

No. 2.—Leaving B. Buoy No. 3, Scraggy Neck Buoy, and Bird Island Buoy on starboard, and return. 10¼ miles.

No. 3.—From starting point, leaving Scraggy Neck Buoy No. 10 on starboard, Wing's Cove Buoy on starboard, Dry Ledge Buoy and Black Buoy No, 3 on port, and return. 11¼ miles.

No. 4.—Reverse of No. 3.

No. 5.—From starting point, leaving Black Buoy No. 3 on starboard, Abial's Ledge Buoy No. 1 on starboard, Dry Ledge Buoy No. 12 on starboard, Black Buoy No. 3 on port, to Judge's Yacht. 7½ miles.

No. 6.—Reverse of No. 5.

No. 7.—Leaving Black Buoy No. 3, Abial's Ledge Buoy, Judge's Yacht, and Black Buoy No. 3 on starboard, to Judge's Yacht. 8¼ miles.

No. 8.—Leaving Black Buoy No. 3, Judge's Yacht, and Black Buoy No. 3 on starboard, to Judge's Yacht. 5 miles.

No 9.—Leaving B. Buoy No. 3 on starboard and return. 2½ miles.

No. 10.—Leaving Black Buoy No. 3, Dry Ledge Buoy No. 12 and Black Buoy No. 3 on starboard, to Judge's Yacht. 7¼ miles.

No. 11.—Leaving Dry Ledge Buoy No. 12 on starboard to Judge's Yacht. 6½ miles.

TABLE OF ALLOWANCE PER MILE.

Length. ft.	in.	Allowance. min.	sec.	Length. ft.	in.	Allowance. min.	sec.
40		0	0.0	37	11	0	7.6
39	11	0	0.3	37	10	0	7.9
39	10	0	0.6	37	9	0	8.2
39	9	0	0.9	37	8	0	8.5
39	8	0	1.2	37	7	0	8.8
39	7	0	1.5	37	6	0	9.2
39	6	0	1.8	37	5	0	9.5
39	5	0	2.1	37	4	0	9.8
39	4	0	2.4	37	3	0	10.1
39	3	0	2.7	37	2	0	10.4
39	2	0	3.0	37	1	0	10.7
39	1	0	3.3	37		0	11.1
39		0	3.6	36	11	0	11.4
38	11	0	3.9	36	10	0	11.7
38	10	0	4.2	36	9	0	12.0
38	9	0	4.5	36	8	0	12.3
38	8	0	4.8	36	7	0	12.7
38	7	0	5.1	36	6	0	13.1
38	6	0	5.4	36	5	0	13.4
38	5	0	5.7	36	4	0	13.7
38	4	0	6.0	36	3	0	14.0
38	3	0	6.3	36	2	0	14.3
38	2	0	6.6	36	1	0	14.7
38	1	0	6.9	36		0	15.1
38		0	7.3	35	11	0	15.4

TABLE OF ALLOWANCE PER MILE—*Continued.*

Length. ft.	in.	Allowance. min.	sec.	Length. ft.	in.	Allowance. min.	sec.
35	10	0	15.7	33	9	0	24.5
35	9	0	16.0	33	8	0	24.9
35	8	0	16.3	33	7	0	25.3
35	7	0	16.7	33	6	0	25.7
35	6	0	17.1	33	5	0	26.0
35	5	0	17.4	33	4	0	26.3
35	4	0	17.7	33	3	0	26.7
35	3	0	18.0	33	2	0	27.1
35	2	0	18.4	33	1	0	27.5
35	1	0	18.8	33		0	27.9
35		0	19.2	32	11	0	28.2
34	11	0	19.5	32	10	0	28.6
34	10	0	19.8	32	9	0	29.0
34	9	0	20.1	32	8	0	29.4
34	8	0	20.5	32	7	0	29.8
34	7	0	20.9	32	6	0	30.2
34	6	0	21.3	32	5	0	30.5
34	5	0	21.6	32	4	0	30.9
34	4	0	21.9	32	3	0	31.3
34	3	0	22.3	32	2	0	31.7
34	2	0	22.7	32	1	0	32.1
34	1	0	23.1	32		0	32.5
34		0	23.5	31	11	0	32.9
33	11	0	23.8	31	10	0	33.3
33	10	0	24.1	31	9	0	33.7

TABLE OF ALLOWANCE PER MILE—*Continued.*

Length. ft.	in.	Allowance. min.	sec.	Length. ft.	in.	Allowance. min.	sec.
31	8	0	34.1	29	7	0	44.5
31	7	0	34.5	29	6	0	45.0
31	6	0	34.9	29	5	0	45.4
31	5	0	35.3	29	4	0	45.8
31	4	0	35.7	29	3	0	46.3
31	3	0	36.1	29	2	0	46.7
31	2	0	36.5	29	1	0	47.1
31	1	0	36.9	29		0	47.6
31		0	37.4	28	11	0	48.0
30	11	0	37.8	28	10	0	48.5
30	10	0	38.2	28	9	0	49.0
30	9	0	38.6	28	8	0	49.4
30	8	0	39.0	28	7	0	49.9
30	7	0	39.4	28	6	0	50.4
30	6	0	39.9	28	5	0	50.8
30	5	0	40.3	28	4	0	51.3
30	4	0	40.7	28	3	0	51.8
30	3	0	41.1	28	2	0	52.2
30	2	0	41.5	28	1	0	52.7
30	1	0	41.9	28		0	53.2
30		0	42.4	27	11	0	53.6
29	11	0	42.8	27	10	0	54.1
29	10	0	43.2	27	9	0	54.6
29	9	0	43.7	27	8	0	55.0
29	8	0	44.1	27	7	0	55.5

TABLE OF ALLOWANCE PER MILE.—*Continued.*

Length. ft.	in.	Allowance. min.	sec.	Length. ft.	in.	Allowance. min.	sec.
27	6	0	56.0	25	5	1	8.7
27	5	0	56.5	25	4	1	9.2
27	4	0	57.0	25	3	1	9.8
27	3	0	57.5	25	2	1	10.3
27	2	0	58.0	25	1	1	10.8
27	1	0	58.5	25		1	11.4
27		0	59.0	24	11	1	11.9
26	11	0	59.5	24	10	1	12.5
26	10	1		24	9	1	13.1
26	9	1	0.5	24	8	1	13.6
26	8	1	1.0	24	7	1	14.2
26	7	1	1.5	24	6	1	14.8
26	6	1	2.0	24	5	1	15.3
26	5	1	2.5	24	4	1	15.9
26	4	1	3.0	24	3	1	16.5
26	3	1	3.5	24	2	1	17.0
26	2	1	4.0	24	1	1	17.6
26	1	1	4.5	24		1	18.2
26		1	5.0	23	11	1	18.7
25	11	1	5.5	23	10	1	19.3
25	10	1	6.0	23	9	1	19.9
25	9	1	6.6	23	8	1	20.5
25	8	1	7.1	23	7	1	21.1
25	7	1	7.6	23	6	1	21.7
25	6	1	8.2	23	5	1	22.3

TABLE OF ALLOWANCE PER MILE.—Continued.

Length. ft.	in.	Allowance. min.	sec.	Length. ft.	in.	Allowance. min.	sec.
23	4	1	22.9	21	3	1	38.9
23	3	1	23.5	21	2	1	39.5
23	2	1	24.1	21	1	1	40.2
23	1	1	24.7	21		1	40.9
23		1	25.3	20	11	1	41.6
22	11	1	25.9	20	10	1	42.3
22	10	1	26.5	20	9	1	43.0
22	9	1	27.2	20	8	1	43.7
22	8	1	27.8	20	7	1	44.4
22	7	1	28.4	20	6	1	45.1
22	6	1	29.1	20	5	1	45.8
22	5	1	29.7	20	4	1	46.5
22	4	1	30.3	20	3	1	47.3
22	3	1	31.0	20	2	1	48.0
22	2	1	31.6	20	1	1	48.7
22	1	1	32.2	20		1	49.5
22		1	32.9	19	11	1	50.2
21	11	1	33.5	19	10	1	50.9
21	10	1	34.2	19	9	1	51.7
21	9	1	34.9	19	8	1	52.4
21	8	1	35.5	19	7	1	53.2
21	7	1	36.2	19	6	1	54.0
21	6	1	36.9	19	5	1	54.7
21	5	1	37.5	19	4	1	55.5
21	4	1	38.2	19	3	1	56.3

TABLE OF ALLOWANCE PER MILE—*Continued*.

Length. ft.	in.	Allowance. min.	sec.	Length. ft.	in.	Allowance. min.	sec.
19	2	1	57.0	17	1	2	18.1
19	1	1	57.8	17		2	19.0
19		1	58.6	16	11	2	19.9
18	11	1	59.4	16	10	2	20.8
18	10	2	0.2	16	9	2	21.8
18	9	2	1.0	16	8	2	22.7
18	8	2	1.8	16	7	2	23.6
18	7	2	2.6	16	6	2	24.6
18	6	2	3.5	16	5	2	25.5
18	5	2	4.3	16	4	2	26.5
18	4	2	5.1	16	3	2	27.5
18	3	2	6.0	16	2	2	28.5
18	2	2	6.8	16	1	2	29.5
18	1	2	7.6	16		2	30.5
18		2	8.5	15	11	2	31.5
17	11	2	9.3	15	10	2	32.5
17	10	2	10.1	15	9	2	33.5
17	9	2	11.0	15	8	2	34.5
17	8	2	11.8	15	7	2	35.5
17	7	2	12.7	15	6	2	36.6
17	6	2	13.6	15	5	2	37.6
17	5	2	14.5	15	4	2	38.6
17	4	2	15.4	15	3	2	39.7
17	3	2	16.3	15	2	2	40.7
17	2	2	17.2	15	1	2	41.8

TIDE TABLES.

HIGH WATER.—STANDARD TIME.

JUNE.

DATE.	MARBLEHEAD.				MONUMENT BEACH.			
	A. M.		P. M.		A. M.		P. M.	
	h.	m.	h.	m.	h.	m.	h.	m.
June 1........	3	16	4	11	0	39	1	00
" 2........	4	16	5	12	1	23	1	45
" 3........	5	19	6	06	2	06	2	27
4........	6	20	6	55	2	49	3	10
5........	7	17	7	39	3	32	3	53
6........	8	07	8	17	4	15	4	37
7........	8	51	8	53	4	59	5	22
8........	9	31	9	29	5	45	6	09
9........	10	07	10	06	6	32	6	56
10........	10	44	10	45	7	19	7	44
11........	11	21	11	24	8	09	8	35
12........	11	59	..	..	9	00	9	26
13........	0	07	12	39	9	54	10	20
14........	12	52	1	25	10	47	11	12
15........	1	39	2	15	11	38	..	..
16........	2	32	3	08	0	02	12	27
17........	3	27	4	04	0	50	1	15
18........	4	26	5	01	1	39	2	04
19........	5	27	6	00	2	29	2	55
20........	6	27	6	56	3	22	3	50
21........	7	29	7	52	4	19	4	48
22........	8	28	8	46	5	19	5	50
23........	9	26	10	31	6	20	6	49
24........	10	22	11	25	7	19	7	48
25........	11	16	12	12	8	16	8	45
26........	..	..	1	03	9	12	9	40
27........	0	16	1	03	10	05	10	31
28........	1	06	1	54	10	55	11	19
29........	1	57	2	44	11	40	..	..
30........	2	49	3	34	0	01	12	22

TIDE TABLES.—*Continued.*

HIGH WATER.—STANDARD TIME.

JULY.

Date.	MARBLEHEAD.				MONUMENT BEACH.			
	A. M.		P. M.		A. M.		P. M.	
	h.	m.	h.	m.	h.	m.	h.	m.
July 1.............	3	43	4	24	0	41	1	01
" 2.............	4	39	5	13	1	21	1	42
" 3.............	5	33	5	59	2	02	2	23
4.............	6	29	6	45	2	45	3	07
5.............	7	23	7	30	3	30	3	55
6.............	8	12	8	15	4	20	4	46
7.............	8	57	8	59	5	12	5	39
8.............	9	39	9	42	6	07	6	34
9.............	10	21	10	25	7	01	7	27
10.............	11	01	11	09	7	53	8	19
11.............	11	42	11	53	8	45	9	10
12.............	..	..	12	25	9	36	10	01
13.............	12	39	1	11	10	26	10	51
14.............	1	26	1	59	11	15	11	39
15.............	2	27	2	49	..	..	12	02
16.............	3	09	3	42	0	26	12	48
17.............	4	06	4	39	1	13	1	37
18.............	5	04	5	36	2	04	2	31
19.............	6	09	6	36	3	00	3	30
20.............	7	15	7	36	4	02	4	33
21.............	8	21	8	36	5	06	5	38
22.............	9	24	9	31	6	09	6	39
23.............	10	19	10	24	7	07	7	34
24.............	11	10	11	14	8	01	8	25
25.............	11	57	..	..	8	49	9	13
26.............	0	01	12	42	9	35	9	57
27.............	12	46	1	24	10	18	10	39
28.............	1	31	2	04	10	59	11	19
29.............	2	16	2	46	11	39	11	57
30.............	3	02	3	29	..	..	12	17
" 31.............	3	50	4	14	0	37	12	57

TIDE TABLES.—*Continued.*
HIGH WATER.—*STANDARD TIME.*
AUGUST.

Date.	Marblehead.		Monument Beach.	
	A. M.	P. M.	A. M.	P. M.
	h. m.	h. m.	h. m.	h. m.
Aug. 1	4 41	5 00	1 18	1 40
" 2	5 35	5 50	2 03	2 27
" 3	6 31	6 42	2 52	3 20
4	7 26	7 34	3 47	4 17
5	8 19	8 26	4 46	5 16
6	9 07	9 16	5 45	6 14
7	9 54	10 04	6 42	7 09
8	10 37	10 51	7 35	8 01
9	11 21	11 36	8 24	8 49
10	.. ..	12 04	9 13	9 37
11	0 22	12 49	10 01	10 24
12	1 09	1 36	10 48	11 12
13	1 58	2 25	11 37	.. ..
14	2 49	3 17	12 01	12 26
15	3 45	4 13	0 52	1 19
16	4 51	5 13	1 48	2 17
17	5 59	6 17	2 49	3 20
18	7 09	7 25	3 53	4 26
" 19	8 19	8 27	4 57	5 28
20	9 20	9 23	5 57	6 25
21	10 13	10 14	6 50	7 14
22	10 58	10 59	7 36	7 59
23	11 38	11 41	8 19	8 39
24	.. ..	12 14	8 58	9 18
25	0 21	12 48	9 37	9 56
26	1 03	1 23	10 16	10 35
27	1 42	1 59	10 58	11 15
28	2 22	2 38	11 36	11 57
29	3 04	3 21	.. ..	12 19
30	3 51	4 09	0 41	1 05
" 31	4 43	5 03	1 29	1 56

TIDE TABLES.—*Continued.*
HIGH WATER.—STANDARD TIME.
SEPTEMBER.

		MARBLEHEAD.				MONUMENT BEACH.			
DATE.		A. M.		P. M.		A. M.		P. M.	
		h.	m.	h.	m.	h.	m.	h.	m.
Sept.	1	5	41	6	01	2	23	2	52
"	2	6	41	6	59	3	21	3	52
"	3	7	41	7	56	4	23	4	52
	4	8	34	8	49	5	22	5	52
	5	9	24	9	41	6	19	6	45
	6	10	10	10	29	7	10	7	34
	7	10	55	11	26	7	59	8	21
	8	11	41	..	..	8	45	9	08
	9	0	03	12	25	9	32	9	57
	10	12	49	1	11	10	23	10	49
	11	1	39	2	01	11	15	11	44
	12	2	31	2	54	..	..	12	11
	13	3	28	3	51	0	40	1	09
	14	4	33	4	55	1	39	2	10
	15	5	48	6	04	2	41	3	13
	16	7	06	7	10	3	43	1	14
	17	8	13	8	18	4	41	5	10
	18	9	09	9	11	5	35	6	00
	19	9	56	10	01	6	22	6	44
	20	10	35	10	44	7	04	7	23
	21	11	09	11	21	7	43	8	02
	22	11	41	11	57	8	20	8	39
	23	..	..	12	11	8	57	9	16
	24	0	32	12	43	9	36	9	56
	25	1	07	1	17	10	20	10	39
	26	1	44	1	54	11	02	11	24
	27	2	24	2	38	11	49	..	..
	28	3	09	3	26	0	13	12	39
	29	4	01	4	22	1	04	1	32
	30	5	01	5	23	2	00	2	28

TIDE TABLES.—*Continued.*

HIGH WATER.—STANDARD TIME.
OCTOBER.

Date.	MARBLEHEAD.		MONUMENT BEACH.	
	A. M.	P. M.	A. M.	P. M.
	h. m.	h. m.	h. m.	h. m.
Oct. 1.............	6 04	6 26	2 57	3 28
" 2.............	7 04	7 26	3 57	4 26
" 3.............	8 00	8 22	4 55	5 21
4.............	8 51	9 15	5 49	6 15
5.............	9 41	10 06	6 39	7 04
6.............	10 27	10 53	7 28	7 52
7.............	11 14	11 41	8 16	8 42
8.............	.. ..	12 00	9 07	9 35
9.............	0 30	12 47	10 03	10 32
10.............	1 20	1 39	11 02	11 32
11.............	2 15	2 33	.. ..	12 02
12.............	3 15	3 32	0 32	1 02
13.............	4 24	4 39	1 31	2 00
14.............	5 39	5 51	2 28	2 57
15.............	6 52	6 59	3 23	3 49
16.............	7 54	8 01	4 15	4 39
17.............	8 45	8 56	5 02	5 24
18.............	9 27	9 41	5 45	6 06
19.............	10 04	10 23	6 26	6 45
20.............	10 36	10 59	7 05	7 23
21.............	11 05	11 32	7 42	8 02
22.............	11 35	.. ..	8 21	8 41
23.............	0 04	12 06	9 03	9 24
24.............	0 37	12 41	9 48	10 11
25.............	1 13	1 20	10 36	11 01
26.............	1 52	2 04	11 27	11 52
27.............	2 39	2 54	.. ..	12 19
28.............	3 31	3 51	0 44	1 11
29.............	3 29	4 51	1 37	2 04
30.............	5 31	5 54	2 31	2 58
31.............	6 31	6 56	3 25	3 53

LIST OF REGATTAS

OF THE

BEVERLY YACHT CLUB.

1891.

At the three regular Club regattas, a champion pennant was awarded in each class to the yacht making the best actual time, to be held till the next race, and at the end of the season to become the property of the yacht winning them the greatest number of times.

At the Club races at Monument Beach, a champion pennant of Buzzard's Bay was given in each class in a similar manner, for best actual time.

All distances given in nautical miles.

Varying lengths are accounted for by changes of Rig.

For numbers of courses. refer to page 37-39.

ONE HUNDRED AND SEVENTIETH REGATTA.

FIRST OPEN SWEEPSTAKES.

MONUMENT BEACH, JUNE 17, 1891.

COURSES—1, 7 AND 9.

Wind, N. E.; very strong.

Name.	Club.	Owner.	Length. ft. in.	Actual Time. h. m. s.	Corrected Time. h. m. s.
		First Class.			
Mattie	B. Y. C.	Howard Stockton	28 10	2 5 15	1 56 58
Hector	Sip. Y. C.	E. C. Stetson	28 10	2 8 28	2 0 11
		Second Class.			
Mist	B. Y. C.	G. H. Lyman, Jr.	26 8	2 0 55	1 50 30
Widgeon	B. Y. C.	Moses Williams, Jr.	26 10	2 3 47	1 53 22
Anonyma	B. Y. C.	F. L. Dabney	26 10	2 6 2	1 55 47
Surprise	B. Y. C.	Jas. M. Codman	27 4	2 9 22	1 59 38
		Third Class.			
Eina	B. Y. C.	John Parkinson	22 10	1 46 31	1 34 37
Phenomenon	B. B. Y. C.	N. Huckins, Jr.	23	1 48 54	1 37 2
Tycoon	B. Y. C.	J. L. Stackpole, Jr.	23 1	1 49 26	1 37 47
Puzzle	B. Y. C.	Wm. Amory, 2d	22 9	Withdrew.	
Daisy	B. Y. C.	Howard Stockton	21 1	"	
Parole	B. Y. C.	W. H. Davis	22 8	"	
Hermione	B. Y. C.	R. L. Barstow	23	"	
Marion	B. B. Y. C.	Geo. Jones	22 5	"	
		Fourth Class.			
Edith	B. Y. C.	G. Van Rensselaer	19 4	Withdrew.	

First Class........ ....1st prize won by Mattie.
Second " ....1st   "   "   Mist.
  "   "   ....2d   "   "   Widgeon.
Third   .... 1st   "   "   Eina.
  "   ' .... 2d   "   "   Phenomenon.
  "   "   .... 3d   "   "   Tycoon.

JUDGES: T. S. EDMANDS, W. LLOYD JEFFRIES.

ONE HUNDRED AND SEVENTY-FIRST REGATTA.

SECOND OPEN SWEEPSTAKES.

MARBLEHEAD, JUNE 26, 1891.

COURSE—5.

Wind, good N. E. breeze at start; calm at finish.

NAME.	CLUB.	OWNER.	Length.		Actual Time.	Corrected Time.
			ft.	in.	h. m. s	h. m. s.
		THIRD CLASS SLOOPS.				
Kraken	B. Y. C.	Percy Chase	26	6	2 19 15	2 11 30
Wraith	B. Y. C.	H. P. Benson	22	3	2 29 45	2 18 22

Kraken—wins.

JUDGE: W. LLOYD JEFFRIES.

ONE HUNDRED AND SEVENTY-SECOND REGATTA.

THIRD OPEN SWEEPSTAKES.
MONUMENT BEACH, JULY 4, 1891.
COURSES—2, 7 AND 9.
Wind, S. W.; two reef breeze.

Name.	Club or Port.	Owner.	Length. ft. in.	Actual Time. h. m. s.	Corrected Time. h. m. s.
		First Class.			
Hector	B. B. Y. C.	E. C. Stetson	28 10	2 2 3	1 53 46
Mattie	B. Y. C.	Howard Stockton	28 10	2 3 34	1 55 17
		Second Class.			
Anonyma	B. Y. C.	F. L. Dabney	27 1	1 56 45	1 46 45
Surprise	B. Y. C.	Jas. M. Codman	27 4	2 0 0	1 50 16
Mollie	Mon. Beach	Fred. Packard	27	2 0 55	1 50 50
Mist	B. Y. C.	Geo. H. Lyman, Jr.	26 8	2 2 26	1 52 1
Widgeon	B. Y. C.	Moses Williams, Jr.	26 10	2 2 42	1 52 27
Crawford	H. C. Y. C.	H. F. Crawford	27 3	2 15 24	2 5 35
Moccasin	B. Y. C.	A. A. Beebe	24	2 29 20	2 15 58
Bonita	B. Y. C.	J. D. Parker	25 9	Did not start	
		Third Class.			
Puzzle	B Y. C.	Wm. Amory, 2d	22 9	1 49 8	1 37 9
Parole	B. Y. C.	W. H. Davis	22 8	1 52 30	1 40 26
Buzzard	B. Y. C.	A. B. Shepley	23 8	1 54 7	1 43 3
Eina	B. Y. C.	John Parkinson	22 10	1 54 34	1 42 40
Tycoon	B. Y. C.	J. L. Stackpole, Jr.	23 1	1 54 48	1 43 9
Ashantee	B. Y. C.	Geo. Pillsbury	23 3	1 55 10	1 43 41
Phenomenon	B. B. Y. C.	N. Huckins, Jr.	23	1 55 39	1 43 55
Hermione	B. Y. C.	R. L. Barstow	23	Withdrew	
		Fourth Class.			
Cat	B. Y. C.	Bruce Clark	19 3	1 18 50	1 9 8
Squall	B. Y. C.	John G. Palfrey	19 11	1 24 22	1 15 11
Edith	B. Y. C.	G. Van Rensselaer	19 4	Did not start	

First Class............1st prize won by Hector.
Second " ....1st " " Anonyma.
   "   " ....2d " " Suprise.
   "   ....3d " " Mollie.
Third   ....1st " " Puzzle.
   " ....2d " " Parole.
   "   " ....3d " " Eina.
Fourth " ....1st " " Cat.

JUDGES: T. S. EDMANDS, W. LLOYD JEFFRIES.

ONE HUNDRED AND SEVENTY-THIRD REGATTA.

FIRST BUZZARD'S BAY CHAMPIONSHIP.

MONUMENT BEACH, JULY 18, 1891.

COURSES—4, 6 AND 12.

Wind, S. E. ; good wholesail breeze.

Name.	Owner.	Length.		Actual Time.			Corrected Time.		
		ft.	in.	h.	m.	s.	h.	m.	s.
	FIRST CLASS.								
Mattie	Howard Stockton	28	10	2	7	46	1	57	50
	SECOND CLASS.								
Mist	Geo. H. Lyman, Jr	26	8	2	12	39	2	1	13
Anonyma	F. L. Dabney	27	1	2	13	49	2	2	51
Widgeon	Moses Williams, Jr	26	10	2	15	50	2	4	35
Bonita	J. D. Parker	25	4	2	18	58	2	5	59
	THIRD CLASS.								
Puzzle	Wm. Amory, 2d	22	9	1	31	49	1	20	55
Eina	John Parkinson	22	10	1	32	40	1	21	51
Cayuse	F. W. Sargent	22	9	1	36	21	1	25	27
Daisy	Howard Stockton	21	1		With	drew.			
	FOURTH CLASS.								
Cat	Bruce Clark	19	3	1	30	35	1	17	1
Edith	G Van Rensselaer	19	4	1	33	56	1	20	57
Squall	John G. Palfrey	19	11	1	34	55	1	22	4

First Class............1st prize won by Mattie.
Second " ....1st " " Mist.
" " ....2d " " Anonyma.
Third ....1st " " Puzzle.
" ' ....2d " " Eina.
Fourth " ....1st " " Cat.

Mattie, Mist, Puzzle and Cat won legs for pennants.

JUDGES: T. S. EDMANDS, F. TUDOR, JR.

ONE HUNDRED AND SEVENTY-FOURTH REGATTA.

FIRST CHAMPIONSHIP.

MARBLEHEAD, AUGUST 1, 1891.

COURSES—3 AND 4.

Wind, light ; S. W.

Name.	Owner.	Length.		Actual Time.			Corrected Time.		
		ft.	in	h.	m.	s.	h.	m.	s.
	First Class.								
Hawk	Gordon Dexter	38	6	2	8	33	2	7	39
	Third Class Sloops.								
Hornet	H. P. Benson	26	3	1	33	10	1	25	31
Kraken	Percy Chase	26	3	1	42	23	1	34	54
	Third Class Cats.								
Kiowa	W. Lloyd Jeffries	22	7	1	40	32	1	29	44
Wanda	R. C. Robbins	22	9	1	42	56	1	32	17
	Fourth Class.								
Marchioness	C. E. Hodges			1	50	55			

First Class.....1st prize and leg for pennant won by Hawk.

Third Class Sloops...1st prize and leg for pennant won by................................Hornet.

Third Class Cats....1st prize and leg for pennant won by.................................Kiowa.

Fourth Class..1st prize and leg for pennant won by Marchioness.

JUDGE: F. ELLIOT CABOT.

ONE HUNDRED AND SEVENTY-FIFTH REGATTA.

FOURTH OPEN SWEEPSTAKES.
MONUMENT BEACH, AUGUST 8, 1891.
COURSES—3, 6 AND 12.

Wind, moderate to calm, shifting all round the compass.

NAME.	CLUB.	OWNER.	Length. ft. in.	Actual Time. h. m. s.	Corrected Time. h. m. s.
		FIRST CLASS.			
Hector.......	Sip. Y. C...	E. C. Stetson	28 10	2 41 55	2 32 49
Mattie........	B. Y. C...	Howard Stockton..	28 10	. Withdrew.	
		SECOND CLASS.			
Surprise.......	B. Y. C ...	Jas. M. Codman....	27 4	2 51 21	2 41 40
Mist	B. Y. C....	Geo. H. Lyman, Jr.	26 8	3 3 33	2 52 7
Anonyma ...	B. Y. C....	F. L. Dabney...	27 1	3 5 2	2 54 4
Widgeon....	B. Y. C....	Moses Williams, Jr.	26 10	3 6 51	2 55 36
Grampus	B. Y. C....	W. E. C. Eustis....	27 9	Withdrew.	
Crawford	H. C. Y. C.	H. Crawford	27 3	Withdrew.	
		THIRD CLASS.			
Eina.........	B. Y. C....	John Parkinson	22 10	1 42 36	1 31 47
Puzzle........	B. Y. C...	Wm. Amory, 2d....	22 9	1 43 35	1 32 41
Phenomenon.	B. B. Y. C	D. L. Whittemore .	23	1 44 43	1 34 3
Parole........	B Y. C...	W. H. Davis.	22 8	1 50 48	1 39 49
Ashantee.....	B. Y. C...	Geo. Pillsbury	23 3	1 53 32	1 43 6
		FOURTH CLASS.			
Cat	B. Y. C....	Bruce Clark........	19 3	1 45 26	1 31 52
Edith	B. Y. C....	G van Rensselaer..	19 4	1 46 56	1 33 27
Charmion....	B. Y. C....	J. Crane. Jr	19 6	1 47 3	1 33 45
Squall.......	B. Y. C....	John G. Palfrey ...	19 11	1 51 57	1 39 6

First Class.............1st prize won by Hector.
Second Class .... 1st " " Surprise.
" " ....2d " " Mist.
" " ....3d " " Anonyma.
Third " ....1st " " Eina.
" " ....2d " " Puzzle.
" " ....3d " " Phenomenon.
Fourth " ....1st " " Cat.
" - ....2d " " Edith.

JUDGES: A. H. HARDY, F. ELLIOT CABOT, W. LLOYD JEFFRIES.

ONE HUNDRED AND SEVENTY-SIXTH REGATTA.

SECOND CHAMPIONSHIP.

MARBLEHEAD, AUGUST 15, 1891.

COURSE—7.

Wind, N. E. strong to moderating, heavy rain and sea.

Name.	Owner.	Length ft in.	Actual Time. h. m. s.	Corrected Time. h. m. s.
	THIRD CLASS CATS.			
Wanda	R. C. Robbins	22 9	1 40 8	1 29 29

Wins prize and ties Kiowa for pennant.

Kiowa and Hawk were on hand, but Hawk declined to walkover, and Kiowa was dismasted just before the start.

JUDGE : MR. WEDGES.

ONE HUNDRED AND SEVENTY-SEVENTH REGATTA.

SECOND BUZZARD'S BAY CHAMPIONSHIP.

MONUMENT BEACH, AUGUST 29, 1891.

COURSES—1, 5 AND 5.

Wind, very moderate, W. to W. S. W.

Name.	Owner.	Length. ft. in	Actual Time. h. m. s.	Corrected Time. h. m. s.
	SECOND CLASS.			
Surprise	Jas. M. Codman	27 4	2 11 53	2 1 26
Mist	Geo. H. Lyman	26 8	2 13 17	2 2 7
Anonyma	F. L. Dabney	27 1	2 13 21	2 2 38
Widgeon	Moses Williams, Jr	26 10	2 20 54	2 9 54
Grampus	W. E. C. Eustis	27 9	2 20 19	2 10 19
	THIRD CLASS.			
Puzzle	Wm. Amory, 2d	22 9	1 57 59	1 47 5
Cayuse	F. W. Sargent	22 9	1 58 18	1 47 19
Buzzard	A. B. Shepley	23 8	1 58 31	1 48 27
Eina	John Parkinson	22 10	1 58 34	1 47 46
	FOURTH CLASS.			
Edith	G. Van Rensselaer	19 4	2 1 37	1 47 11
Cat	Bruce Clark	19 3	2 7 26	1 52 54
Squall	John G. Palfrey	19 11	2 17 34	2 3 48
Charmion	Joshua Crane, Jr	19 6	Withdrew	
Kitten	Tobey Club	19 11	Withdrew	
Duckling	Roger S. Hardy	17 9	Withdrew	

Second Class..............1st prize won by Surprise.
    "   "..............2d "   " Mist.
Third   "..............1st "   " Puzzle.
   "..............2d "   " Cayuse.
Fourth "..............1st " Edith.
   "..............2d "   " Cat.
Second " leg for pennant won by Surprise tieing Mist.
Third " leg for pennant won and held by Puzzle.
Fourth " leg for pennant won by Edith tieing Cat.

JUDGE: A. H. HARDY.

ONE HUNDRED AND SEVENTY-EIGHTH REGATTA.

FIFTH OPEN SWEEPSTAKES.

MARBLEHEAD, SEPTEMBER 5, 1891.

COURSE—1.

Wind, good, N. E. at start, shifting to E. and moderating.

NAME.	OWNER.	Length.		Actual Time.			Corrected Time.		
		ft.	in.	h.	m.	s.	h.	m.	s
	FIRST CLASS.								
Fancy	C. F. Lyman,	38		2	15	50	2	14	37
Hawk	Gordon Dexter	38	7	2	22	21	2	20	31

Won by Fancy.

JUDGE: F. ELLIOT CABOT.

ONE HUNDRED AND SEVENTY-NINTH REGATTA.

OPEN RACE.

MONUMENT BEACH, SEPTEMBER 7, 1891.

COURSES—2 AND 7.

Wind, severe N. E. gale, blinding rain, very thick.

Name.	Club or Port.	Owner.	Length. ft. in.	Actual Time. h. m. s.	Corrected Time. h. m. s.
Second Class.					
Anonyma	B. Y. C.	F. L. Dabney	27 1	2 3 7	1 53 7
Defiance	Mon. Beach	H. E. Perry	26 4	2 3 45	1 52 59
Surprise	B. Y. C.	Jas. M. Codman	27 4	2 6 31	1 55 47
Widgeon	B. Y. C.	Moses Williams, Jr.	26 10	Withdrew	
Third Class.					
Parole	B. Y. C.	W. H. Davis	22 8	2 4 17	1 52 13
Puzzle	B. Y. C.	Wm. Amory, 2d	22 9	2 7 5	1 55 6
Daisy	B. Y. C.	Howard Stockton	21 1	2 12 11	1 58 12
Eina	B. Y. C.	John Parkinson	22 10	Withdrew	

A very large majority of the entries were kept out by the weather.

Second Class............1st prize won by Defiance.
  "   "   ....2d   "   "   Anonyma.
Third   "   ....1st   "   "   Parole.
  "   "   ....2d   "   "   Puzzle.

JUDGE: W. LLOYD JEFFRIES.

ONE HUNDRED AND EIGHTIETH REGATTA.

SIXTH OPEN SWEEPSTAKES.

MONUMENT BEACH, SEPTEMBER 12, 1891.

COURSES—1, 7 AND 9.

Wind, S. W., good wholesail breeze.

Name.	Club or Port.	Owner.	Length ft.	Length in.	Actual h.	m.	s.	Corrected h.	m.	s.
		SECOND CLASS.								
Surprise	B. Y. C.	Jas. M. Codman	27	4	2	5	56	1	56	12
Anonyma	B. Y. C.	F. L. Dabney	27	1	2	6	11	1	56	11
Defiance	Mon. Beach	H. E. Perry	26	4	2	8	15	1	57	29
Mist	B. Y. C.	Geo. H. Lyman	26	8	2	8	21	1	57	56
Widgeon	B. Y. C.	Moses Williams, Jr.	26	10	2	11	48	2	1	33
Wildcat	Mon. Beach	J. N. Norcross	26	4	2	13	25	2	2	39
Grampus	B. Y. C.	W. E. C. Eustis	27	9	With	drew.				
		THIRD CLASS.								
Eina	B. Y. C.	John Parkinson	22	10	1	53	38	1	41	44
Tycoon	B. Y. C.	J. L. Stackpole, Jr.	23	1	1	53	47	1	42	48
Puzzle	B. Y. C.	Wm. Amory, 2d	22	9	1	55	45	1	43	46
Daisy	B. Y. C.	Howard Stockton	21	1	With	drew.				
		FOURTH CLASS.								
Cat	B. Y. C.	Bruce Clark	19	3	1	23	51	1	14	9
Edith	B. Y. C.	G. Van Rensselaer	19	4	1	26	27	1	16	49
Charmion	B. Y. C.	Joshua Crane, Jr.	19	6	1	32	7	1	22	37
Kitten	B. Y. C.	Tobey Club	19	11	1	32	37	1	23	26

Second Class .... 1st prize won by Anonyma.
" " .... 2d " " Surprise.
" .... 3d " Defiance.
Third " .... 1st ' ' Eina.
" .... 2d ' " Tycoon.
Fourth " .... 1st ' Cat.
" .... 2d ' Edith.

JUDGE: T. S. EDMANDS.

ONE HUNDRED AND EIGHTY-FIRST REGATTA.

THIRD CHAMPIONSHIP.

MARBLEHEAD, SEPTEMBER 19, 1891.

COURSE—NO. 6.

Wind, very light, E. by S. to S.

NAME.	OWNER.	Length. ft. in.	Actual Time. h. m. s.	Corrected Time. h. m. s.
	THIRD CLASS CATS.			
Kiowa	W. Lloyd Jeffries	22 7	2 16 28	2 5 25
Wanda	R. C. Robbins	22 9	2 20 4	2 9 46
	THIRD CLASS SLOOPS.			
Kraken	Percy Chase	26 3	2 9 15	2 1 20
	FOURTH CLASS.			
Marchioness	C. E. Hodges.		2 16 6	

Kiowa, Kraken and Marchioness take prizes, Kiowa and Marchioness win and hold pennants. Kraken wins leg for pennants tieing Hornet, and as Hornet was laid up the sail off was postponed till 1892 at the request of Kraken.

JUDGE: F. ELLIOT CABOT.

ONE HUNDRED AND EIGHTY-SECOND REGATTA.

THIRD BUZZARD'S BAY CHAMPIONSHIP.

MONUMENT BEACH, SEPTEMBER 26, 1891.

COURSES—2, 6 AND 9.

Wind, N. E. by N.; single reef at start, whole sail at finish.

Name.	Owner.	Length. ft. in.	Actual Time. h. m. s.	Corrected Time. h. m. s.
	Third Class.			
Violet	Tobey Club	27 6	2 21 41	2 12 7
	Second Class.			
Anonyma	F. L. Dabney	27 1	2 11 12	2 1 12
Surprise	Jas. M. Codman	27 4	2 11 18	2 1 34
Mist	Geo. H. Lyman	26 8	2 15 28	2 5 3
Widgeon	Moses Williams, Jr	26 10	2 17 49	2 7 34
Grampus	W. E. C. Eustis	27 9	2 18 30	2 9 10
	Third Class.			
Eina	John Parkinson	22 10	1 43 15	1 32 26
Daisy	Howard Stockton	21 1	1 45 43	1 33 11
	Fourth Class.			
Cat	Bruce Clark	19 3	1 9 36	0 59 54
Edith	G. Van Rensselaer	19 4	1 10 24	1 1 46
Kitten	Tobey Club	19 11	1 12 19	1 3 8
Charmion	Joshua Crane, Jr	19 6	1 12 36	1 3 6

First Class............1st prize won by Violet.
Second " ....1st   "   "   Anonyma.
  "   " ....2d   "   "   Surprise.
Third   " ....1st   "   "   Eina.
Fourth " ....1st   "   "   Cat.
  "   " ....2d   "   "   Edith.
First   " ...Pennant won by Violet tieing Mattie.
Second " ...   "   "   Anonyma, tieing Mist and Surprise.
Fourth " ...Pennant won and held by Cat.

JUDGES: T. S. EDMANDS, A. H. HARDY.

ONE HUNDRED AND EIGHTY-THIRD REGATTA.

SAIL OFF FOR BUZZARD'S BAY CHAMPIONSHIP.

MONUMENT BEACH, OCTOBER 3, 1891.

COURSE—1.

Wind, S. W.; strong to moderate.

NAME.	OWNER.	Actual Time. h. m. s.
FIRST CLASS.		
Violet	Tobey Club	2 24 22
SECOND CLASS.		
Surprise	Jas. M. Codman	2 9 15
Anonyma	F. L. Dabney	2 9 38
Mist	Geo. H. Lyman	2 9 58

Violet and Surprise won pennants.

CHAMPIONS FOR 1891.

First Class....................Hawk.
Third Class Cats ....Kiowa.
Third Class Sloops............Kraken and Hornet tie.
Fourth Class..................Marchioness.

BUZZARD'S BAY CHAMPIONS FOR 1891.

First Class...................Violet.
Second Class..................Surprise.
Third Class...................Puzzle.
Fourth Class ....Cat.

PRIVATE SIGNALS.

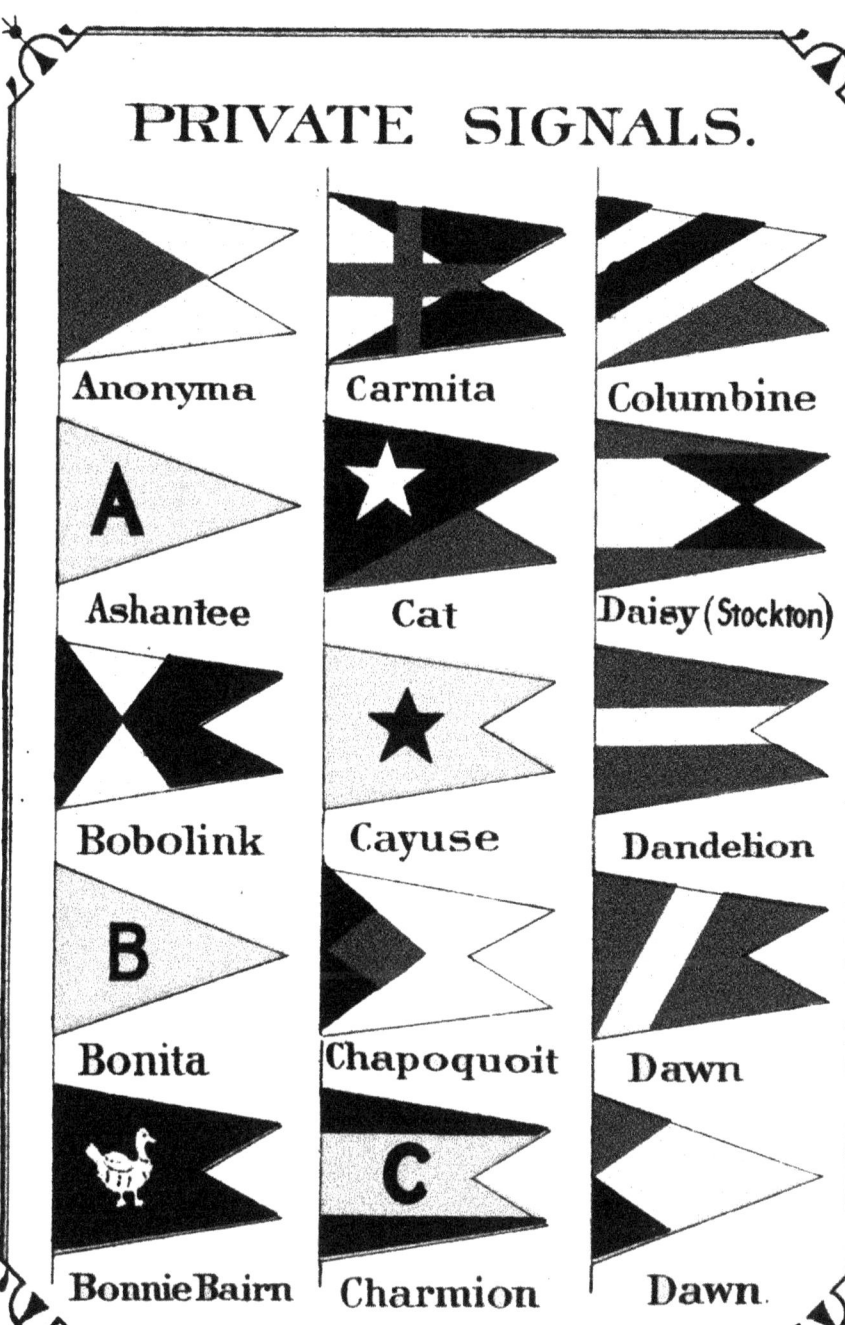